The D-Day Story

The D-Day Story

Martin Bowman

The History Press

Published in the United Kingdom in 2013 by
The History Press
The Mill · Brimscombe Port · Stroud · Gloucestershire · GL5 2QG

British Library Cataloguing in Publication Data
A catalogue record for this book is available from the British
Library.

Hardback ISBN 978-0-7524-9142-4

Typesetting and origination by The History Press
Printed in India

Half title page: 'Mulberry B' (Arromanches) Harbour in
1975. (Author)

Half title verso: 'Pegasus Bridge' near the Café
Gondrée, the first house liberated on D-Day. (Author)

CONTENTS

Title page: A GI helmet washed up on 'Omaha' Beach in the 1990s. (Author/Mick Royall) *'They're murdering us here! Let's move inland and get murdered! '29 - Let's go!'* Brigadier General Norman 'Dutch' Cota, 51-year-old deputy commander 29th Infantry Division, who inspired his troops to breach the sea wall on Omaha Beach. Cota penetrated inland to a point the American frontline as a whole would not reach until two days later.

Left: The 6in gun cruiser HMS *Belfast*, which left the Clyde on 3 June and arrived in the Eastern Task Force at 0500hrs on D-Day. After the Second World War she supported United Nations forces in Korea and remained in service with the Royal Navy until 1965, before being saved for the nation in 1971 and moored opposite the Tower of London. (Author)

In 1942 British Prime Minister Winston Churchill told Lord Louis Mountbatten, Chief of Combined Operations, that unless the Allies could land overwhelming forces 'and beat the Nazis in battle in France, Adolph Hitler would never be defeated. So this must be your prime task.' In spring 1943, at the Anglo-American Trident Conference, the British Chiefs of Staff committed themselves to Operation 'Overlord' – the invasion of Europe – and the Combined Chiefs issued their directive to General Frederick E. Morgan, who had been appointed Chief of Staff to the Supreme Allied Commander (Designate) 'COSSAC', at the Casablanca Conference: 'To mount and carry out an operation, with forces and equipment established in the United Kingdom and with target date 1 May 1944, to secure a lodgement on the Continent from which further offensive operations could be developed. The lodgement area must contain sufficient port facilities to maintain a force of twenty-six to thirty divisions and enable that force to be augmented by follow-up shipments from the United States or elsewhere of additional divisions and supporting units at the rate of three to five divisions per month.'

In August 1943, at the Quebec Summit, the COSSAC plan to invade the Continent in Normandy was approved by Churchill, Roosevelt and the Combined Chiefs of Staff. It was also agreed that the Supreme Commander should be American and that his deputy and three commanders-in-chief should be British, and May 1944 was fixed as the target date. In November 1943 thirty directives for Overlord were issued. During the Tehran Conference at the end of November, Marshal Joseph Stalin, the

➤➤ 'Second Front Now' rally at the Albert Hall in 1943 in support of the Soviet Union.

Soviet dictator, agitated for the opening of the 'second front'. Roosevelt and Churchill promised him that the invasion would start in May 1944. The target date of 1 May for invasion was later postponed for a month to enable extra landing craft to be built, and the initial assault was expanded from three to five Army divisions. Overlord proceeded in London under the direction of General Morgan and Brigadier General R.W. Barker, who set up an Anglo-American headquarters (HQ) to prepare an outline plan for the invasion of North-West Europe from Britain under the direction of the Supreme Commander. On 6 December 1943, 53-year-old American General Dwight D. Eisenhower – known informally as 'Ike' – was appointed to command the landings in France.

Two areas for invasion were considered. The Pas de Calais had many obvious advantages, such as good air support and a quick turnaround for shipping, but it was the most strongly defended area of the whole French coast and did not offer good opportunities for an expansion of the bridgehead. The Caen sector, however, was weakly held; the defences were relatively light, and the beaches were high capacity and sheltered from the prevailing winds. Inland the terrain was suitable for airfield development and for the consolidation of a bridgehead. So the initial landing on the Continent would be in the Caen area, with the eventual seizure of the Cherbourg–Brittany group of ports. Seine Bay, the area of Normandy chosen for the assault, is 50 miles (80km) across and stretches from Barfleur, where William of Normandy set sail for the invasion of England in 1066, eastwards to the mouth of the River Seine. Because it was ultimately intended that American forces should be supplied directly from the United States, their troops

were assigned to the western sector, while the British and Canadian beaches were in the eastern sector. The invasion would require twenty-four different embarkation points spread over 1,000 miles (1,600km) of British coastline, made necessary by

➤ The Allied Commanders at their HQ in Norfolk House, London, in February 1944. *Left to right*: Lieutenant General Omar N. Bradley, Commander US First Army; Admiral Sir Bertram H. Ramsay, Allied Naval Commander; Air Chief Marshal Sir Arthur W. Tedder, Deputy Supreme Commander; General Dwight D. Eisenhower Supreme Commander; General Bernard L. Montgomery, C-in-C Land Forces, CO 21st Army Group; Air Chief Marshal Sir Trafford Leigh-Mallory, C-in-C Allied Expeditionary Air Force (AEAF); and Major General Walter Bedell Smith, Chief of Staff.

➤➤ Map of D-Day.

the total loading capacity in twenty-four hours, since the assault and follow-up had to load simultaneously. The British would load from Great Yarmouth to Portsmouth and the Americans from Southampton to Milford Haven. Each of the twenty-four points required its own embarkation camp, marshalling and concentration area, and

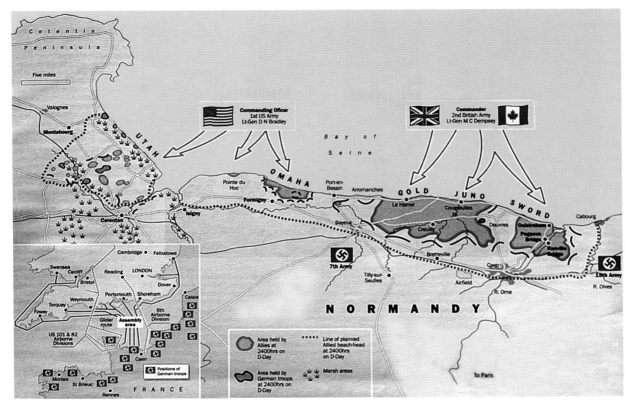

Cotentin Peninsula

Five miles

Valognes

Montebourg

UTAH

Commanding Oficer
1st US Army
Lt-Gen D N Bradley

Carentan

Pointe du Hoc

OMAHA

Formigny

Isigny

Bay of Seine

Port-en-Bessin

Arromanches

Le Hamel

Bayeux

Commander
2nd British Army
Lt-Gen M C Dempsey

GOLD   JUNO   SWORD

Courseulles

Creully

Douvres

Ouistreham

Pegasus Bridge

Ranville Bridge

Cabourg

7th Army

Bretteville

Tilly-sur-Seulles

Caen

Airfield

R. Orne

19th Army

R. Dives

N O R M A N D Y

To Paris

Swansea
Cardiff
Bristol
Torquay
Fowey
Weymouth
Portsmouth
Shoreham
Reading
Cambridge • Felixstowe
LONDON
Dover
Calais
6th Airborne Division
Caen
US 101 & 82 Airborne Divisions
Glider route
Assembly area
Morlaix
St Brieuc
Rennes

F R A N C E

Positions of German troops

Area held by Allies at 2400hrs on D-Day

Area held by German troops at 2400hrs on D-Day

Line of planned Allied beach-head at 2400hrs on D-Day

Marsh areas

11

➤ USS *Texas,* part of the vast Allied armada gathered for D-Day. This battleship, which was the world's most powerful warship when commissioned in 1914 and served with the British Grand Fleet in the First World War, left Belfast Lough at 0215hrs on 3 June for the Western Task Force area.

Between 0550–0625hrs on D-Day, from 10 miles offshore, USS *Texas* fired about 250 14in shells at the six-gun battery at Pointe-du-Hoc, overlooking both Omaha and Utah beaches, before changing targets to fire another 350 shells at the resistance nests on Omaha. She is now displayed at the San Jacinto State Historical Park, 22 miles east of Houston. (Author)

➤➤ St Paul's School, Hammersmith, London, where General Montgomery set up his invasion HQ.

special road layout – many of which had to be either built or greatly improved.

On 1 January 1944 General Sir Bernard Law Montgomery relinquished command of Eighth Army in Italy and flew to England as Commander-in-Chief of Land Forces to set up his invasion HQ at his old school of St Paul's, Hammersmith. 'Monty', as he was affectionately known, had defeated Field Marshal Erwin Rommel's forces at El Alamein in 1942, and now they would lock horns once again. After a brief period in Italy, the 'Desert Fox' had been given command of Army Group B in Northern France in January 1944. Montgomery, whose early ancestors lived in Normandy, would remain in command of 21st Army Group until September when General Eisenhower would assume direct control.

For the purposes of Overlord, Royal Air Force (RAF) Bomber Command and the Eighth US Air Force (USAAF) were placed under the operational direction of the Supreme Commander to add to the aircraft of the Allied Tactical Air Forces. On 17 January Supreme Headquarters, Allied Expeditionary Force (SHAEF) was established in London. Four days later Eisenhower and Monty agreed changes to General Morgan's COSSAC plans, which set the invasion date as 31 May, extending the landing area west across the Cotentin Peninsular towards Cherbourg and increasing the initial seaborne force from three to five divisions. On 1 February the revised Overlord plan, codenamed 'Neptune' (the sea transportation and landing phase of Overlord), was issued.

In April 1944 all leave was cancelled for troops destined for Overlord. The eighteen Allied air forces, including Second Tactical Air Force, RAF Fighter Command and the US 9th (Tactical) Air Force under the direction of Air Chief Marshal Sir Trafford Leigh-Mallory, Air Commander-in-Chief of the Allied Expeditionary Air Force (AEAF), began pre-invasion bombing of France and targets in the Pas de Calais. From the beginning of May the US 9th Air Force dispatched more than a thousand aircraft each day, weather permitting, against railway marshalling yards and important bridges in Northern France.

On the night of 27/28 April, seaborne preparations were dealt a blow during Operation 'Tiger', a realistic US rehearsal for Overlord at Slapton Sands between Plymouth and Dartmouth, when two German E-boats in the English Channel sank two Landing Ship Tanks (LSTs) and damaged others with the loss of 946 men. During 2–6 May, Operation 'Fabius', the final rehearsal for Overlord, was carried out at Slapton Sands. On 1 May Eisenhower

▼ German soldiers stand guard on the Atlantic Wall.

A German propaganda photo showing a heavy gun emplacement in the Wehrmacht's supposedly impregnable Atlantic wall. Massive concrete gun emplacements like these were few and far between and most were situated in the Pas de Calais, Cherbourg and Le Havre.

Did You Know?

On 26 January 1942, Private (first class) Milburn Henke of Hutchison, Minnesota, was the first of 2 million American soldiers to arrive in Britain during the build-up to D-Day. By June 1943, Americans were living in 100,000 buildings in 1,100 locations in Britain. In December, 30,000 further acres of South Devon were taken over and 3,000 residents evicted from 750 properties. Landings were rehearsed in Devon's Bideford Bay, chosen for its similarity to the Normandy coast.

and Admiral Sir Bertram Ramsay, the Allied Naval Commander, aware that Rommel was strengthening the Atlantic Wall (by D-Day, 6½ million mines were laid along the approaches) and covering the beaches with below-the-water obstacles, decided that the landings would be in daylight and at low tide, so that the obstacles would be visible. A daylight landing would also increase the accuracy of air and naval bombardment. On 8 May SHAEF selected 5 June as D-Day. HM King George VI, General Eisenhower and others attended a conference at Montgomery's HQ to review the final plans for Overlord. On 18 May German radio broadcast that 'the invasion would come any day'.

On 23 May camps containing the soldiers landing on D-Day were sealed with barbed wire. On 1 June Admiral Ramsay took command of the immense armada of ships for Operation Neptune. Senior Allied commanders were told that D-Day was

▲ General Eisenhower and his deputy, Air Chief Marshal Sir Arthur Tedder (left), visiting an American unit training in England. (NA)

➤ American Landing Craft Assault s(LCAs), small landing craft capable of carrying an infantry platoon (30–40 troops), being lowered. (USNA)

▲ French guidebook.

Did You Know?
Of the thirty-nine divisions involved in Operation Overlord, twenty were American, fourteen were British, three were Canadian (100,000 men), and France and Poland contributed one division each.

5 June and detailed briefings began. The leading troops were to land (H-Hour) at a few minutes before 0600hrs and after 0700hrs. The Americans were to land first on 'Utah' and 'Omaha' then, minutes later, to allow for the difference in the time of

Plaque on the wall of Norfolk House, commemorating Eisenhower's first London HQ. (Author)

Lance Corporal Collings of the 5th Royal Inniskilling Dragoon Guards consults his French handbook, which was issued to every man taking part in the invasion.

Did You Know?
The US Navy provided 16.5 per cent of the Allied warships and hundreds of landing vessels, and Eighth and Ninth Air Forces fielded 6,080 tactical and strategic aircraft in the Allied Expeditionary Air Force. Britain provided about 80 per cent of the warships. RAF aircraft flew 5,656 sorties.

low tide, the British and Canadians agreed to land on 'Gold', 'Sword' and 'Juno'. Eisenhower and Montgomery moved elements of their HQs to Admiral Ramsay's naval HQ at Southwick House, 10 miles (16km) north-west of Portsmouth, to be near the embarkation ports. Plotting rooms and training facilities were created and temporary accommodation huts, workshops and other buildings were constructed in the extensive grounds. It was in the library near the map room that General Eisenhower made the historic decision to launch D-Day, but on 31 May Group Captain John Stagg, the Chief Meteorological Officer, warned Eisenhower to expect stormy weather for several days to come. Early on Sunday 4 June at Southwick House, Stagg told Ike

◀ B-17G *D-Day Doll* in the 710th Bomb Squadron, 447th Bomb Group, Eighth Air Force at Rattlesden, Suffolk. *Stars and Stripes* gave American losses over Europe in the five months preceding D-Day as 1,407 heavy bombers, 673 fighters and 100 medium bombers. These figures do not include those killed or wounded when the planes returned to their home base or crashed in the UK. Over 14,000 men were lost in the 'heavies' alone. (USAF)

➤ GIs board Landing Craft Infantry (Large) at Weymouth's Portland Harbour. The LCIs were assembled at Dartmouth, the Medway, Newhaven, Portsmouth, Plymouth, Southampton and Weymouth. LCIs were 300ft (90m) long, could carry around 200 assault troops and could land them down gangways lowered on each side of the bow.

‘Building a caisson for Mulberry Harbour' by Muirhead Bone. Up to 45,000 workers in companies all over Britain were involved in the round-the-clock construction of the two 'Mulberries'. These consisted of 4 miles (6.5km) of piers and 6 miles (9.5km) of floating roadway from fifteen pier heads, towed in sections and submerged on D+1. Each enclosed more than 2 square miles (5 square km) of water with a breakwater of concrete caissons, each five storeys high and weighing 6,000 tons. 200,000 tons of old ships known as 'Gooseberries' were towed from Scotland and sunk alongside the 'Mulberries' to act as breakwaters.

◄ 'Phoenix Afloat' by Dwight C. Shepler. (USN Combat Art Collection)

Did You Know?

Because it was thought the retreating Germans would destroy large quantities of French currency, French francs were printed in America. Of these, 2,899,500,000 francs were allotted to the 21st Army Group. On 21 June the Base Cashier landed in France with five and a half tons of notes which were held in the specially reinforced cellars of the Château de Courseulles. The sterling equivalent of £21.7m was sent to France.

➤ B-26B Marauder *Dee-Feater* in the 596th Bomb Squadron, 397th Bomb Group at Rivenhall. Between 12–24 May the 397th was one of the units in the Ninth Air Force that attacked seven German coastal defence targets and continued to do so in the first three days of June, culminating on D-Day with a 'maximum effort' mission in support of the landings in Normandy. (Charles E. Brown)

▲ Field Marshal Erwin Rommel, commanding Army Group B in Northern France.

Did You Know?
Trucks, jeeps, transports and staff cars caused such traffic congestion in the days before D-Day that in Andover, Hampshire, office workers were given fifteen minutes extra at lunchtime to cross the street.

and his eight other senior commanders that the forecast was a rising wind and thicker cloud. His report at 1630hrs was no better: Montgomery was prepared to go despite the weather, but Leigh-Mallory, concerned about the very real threat that a 1,000ft cloud ceiling and gale-force winds would pose to the air forces, was not in favour and urged a postponement. Initially Montgomery disagreed but when Ramsay pointed out that the commanders had to make up their minds within half an hour or it would be too late and the main naval force would have set off, he concurred. With so much depending upon air superiority, Eisenhower had no choice but to postpone the landings for twenty-four hours. All sea-going convoys had to reverse their course and the fleet of big ships steaming south from the Irish Sea turned about to steam north for twelve hours. A flotilla of minesweepers was only 35 miles (56km) from the Normandy coast when it received the order to return. Rommel, convinced an invasion was not imminent, left for Germany to attend his wife's birthday.

Did You Know?

Major General Sir Percy 'Hobo' Hobart's 'Funnies' consisted of bulldozer tanks to clear away beach obstacles; flail tanks to beat pathways through minefields; tanks which could hurl explosive charges against concrete fortifications; turret-less tanks which were, in effect, self-propelled ramps, over which other tanks could scale sea walls; flame-throwing tanks to deal with pillboxes; amphibious or DD (Duplex-Drive) 'swimming' tanks which could swim ashore under their own power; and bridge-carrying tanks to span craters and ditches.

At Southwick House one wall was devoted to a plywood map of the whole of southern Britain, the Channel and Normandy on which the progress of the invasion was to be charted. In May the Midlands toy company, Chad Valley, had been ordered to make a map covering the entire European coastline from Norway to Spain. The two workmen who delivered it were told to erect only the Normandy section and were then held at Southwick until the invasion was under way. The forty or fifty people who worked in the room included members of the Women's Royal Naval Service (WRNS), who plotted the positions of convoys on a huge table. The ships' progress was mapped using chinagraph pencils on Perspex and the plots were frequently updated based on information constantly supplied by radar stations along the coast. The map and the room fell into disuse after D-Day and it was not until after the war that the operations room was restored. (RN)

Did You Know?

Correspondents chosen in great secrecy to go ashore with the troops on D-Day were few. Cornelius Ryan, a *Daily Telegraph* correspondent who later wrote *The Longest Day* and *A Bridge Too Far,* flew in on D-Day. Doon Campbell of Reuters, who was born without a left arm, had filed well-received stories from the bitter fighting at Monte Cassino in February 1944, and was the youngest of the British correspondents who went over on D-Day with Lord Lovat's commando brigade.

At the morning conference on Monday 5 June Stagg predicted thirty-six hours of relatively clear weather with moderate winds. Eisenhower turned to Montgomery and asked whether he could see any reason for not going on Tuesday, to which Montgomery replied: 'I would say – Go!' Ramsay agreed but Leigh-Mallory and Sir Arthur Tedder, Deputy Commander, were unsure. Major General Walter Bedell Smith, Chief of Staff, said: 'It's a helluva gamble, but it's the best possible gamble.' 'OK' said Eisenhower, 'we'll go.' A coded wireless message was sent out by the BBC to instruct the French Resistance to cut railway lines throughout France.

➤ Training For D-Day.

➤➤ A British War Savings poster showing a DUKW amphibious truck, a Landing Craft (Tank) and a Landing Craft (Vehicle, Personnel), a small landing craft which could carry up to forty troops, or twenty Sherman tanks. The main type of LCT used on D-Day was the LST(2) (Landing Ship, Tank) designed by John C. Niedermair and mass produced in the US for the Allied navies.

Did You Know?
Operation 'Bodyguard' misled the enemy about the intentions of the Allies on D-Day. All German agents in Britain were caught and most were 'turned' to transmit misleading information back to their controllers. This 'Double Cross' system under the direction of the XX Committee was designed to confuse the Germans as a key part of Operation 'Fortitude', the most ambitious deception in the history of warfare.

Did You Know?

Misinformation fed to the Germans included a notional '1st US Army Group' under General George S. Patton Jr with '150,000 troops' located on the east coast between the Thames and The Wash. An entire dummy oil-tank farm with mock containers designed by the architect Sir Basil Spence, and made to look as realistic as possible by illusionist Jasper Maskelyne, was erected near Dover. A report given to Hitler at midday on D-Day concluded that a further large-scale operation in the Channel was expected to be made there.

American soldiers in LCIs at Weymouth's Portland Harbour. The barrage balloons are ready to protect the ships against air attack.

Did You Know?

Field Marshal Sir Bernard Law Montgomery (17 November 1887–24 March 1976) had fought on the Western Front in the First World War and been badly wounded and was awarded the Distinguished Service Order (DSO). He returned to France in 1939, commanding the 3rd Division, and took part in the withdrawal to Dunkirk in 1940.

Did You Know?

Nineteen BBC commentators were given combat training and brought to a peak of physical fitness for D-Day. A lightweight disc recorder powered by dry battery, weighing only 40lb and carrying twelve discs which had to be 'cut' on the field of battle, and a microphone that could be clipped on to trees or fences, enabled the reporters to record frontline radio reports. Richard Dimbleby telephoned his report back to London at 1615hrs on 6 June and it was broadcast to an audience of over 15 million listeners huddled around their wireless sets that evening.

◄ M4 Sherman medium tank runs out of a US Navy LST during a stateside training exercise. (USNA)

Did You Know?
SHAEF estimated that about 16,000 Frenchmen and women were under arms and their part in the D-Day operation was crucial.

German intelligence, which had partially broken the code, warned Rommel's HQ at Château de la Roche-Guyon, but in his absence it seems to have been ignored.

During the night of 5/6 June two naval Task Forces (Western and Eastern) totalling 6,203 ships and carrying the force of thirty Army divisions – twenty American, fourteen British, three Canadian, one Free French and one Polish – set sail for Normandy.

Did You Know?

In August 1943, during Churchill's voyage aboard the *Queen Mary* en route to Quebec for the summit with Roosevelt, Professor John Desmond Bernal, a scientific advisor, used a loofah as a wave machine and twenty paper boats as the D-Day fleet. With the prime minister and aides looking on, he proved success would depend on vast floating harbours – 'Mulberries' – represented by a Mae West life preserver.

The armada converged on an area south of the Isle of Wight known unofficially as 'Piccadilly Circus'. At 0500hrs on 6 June the first of the bombarding ships opened fire, the heaviest bombardment taking place during the first fifty minutes after the sun rose at 0558hrs. Their task was to silence, with saturating fire, not only the thirteen main coastal artillery batteries but also the beach defence forces and then, after the assault has gone in, to engage other targets assisted by ground and air spotters. Shipping losses were less than anticipated but casualties to landing and small craft proved higher than allowed for, although 75 per cent of these were attributed to the weather. Three German torpedo boats on patrol sank the Norwegian destroyer *Svenner*, 12 miles (19km) west of Le Havre. A delayed action mine sank the US destroyer *Corry* in the western sector and HMS *Wrestler* suffered mine damage and had to be taken in tow. At 0900hrs the German 84th Corps was informed of seaborne landings. In Britain at 0930hrs the announcement of Overlord was released to the press. Tactical surprise was total.

Inside her cell at Caen prison, Madame Amelie Lechavalier awaited execution. With her husband Louis, who was in the next cell, she had risked her life working secretly in the Allied pilot escape network. On the morning of 6 June a tin plate bearing breakfast was pushed under her door with a whispered message: 'Hope, Hope. The British have landed'. Then came the sound of boots running, cell doors opening and German guards screaming 'Raus, Raus!' The Gestapo guards had set up two machine-guns in the prison courtyard. All the male prisoners were led out, lined against the wall and murdered. There were ninety-two shootings in all – Louis Lechavalier among them.

Did You Know?

The first 'Mulberry' harbour designs were made at Kingswood School in Bath, the codename coming from a tree standing in the grounds. In eight months, two Mulberry harbours made up of 400 units, totalling 1.5 million tons, and five 'Gooseberry' 6,000-ton 'Phoenix' concrete breakwaters were built to deal with up to 12,000 tons of stores and 2,500 vehicles a day, as well as Atlantic storms and dramatic tide differences. From drawing board to construction, Mulberry took less than a fifth of the time it took to build Dover harbour, which had half the capacity.

D-Day began with an assault behind enemy lines between 0115hrs and 0130hrs by more than 23,000 airborne troops – 15,500 in the US 82nd 'All American' and 101st 'Screaming Eagles' airborne divisions – to occupy German defenders and secure the exits from the invasion beaches. The main body of the American airborne divisions who landed by parachute and glider inland of the coast knew that if the accompanying assault by sea failed then there would be no rescue. Departing from Portland Bill on the English Coast, 6,600 paratroopers of the 101st Division, commanded by Major General Maxwell Taylor, in 633 C-47s and 83 gliders, and 6,396 paratroopers of the 82nd Division in 1,101 C-47s and 427 gliders, were dropped over the neck of the Cotentin Peninsula. Night-fighters swept the way clear and heavy cloud covered the approach

➤ A C-47, also known as the 'Skytrain' by the Americans and the 'Dakota' by the British, casts its silhouette on the ground. It was primarily used for parachute drops and as a glider tug. (Author)

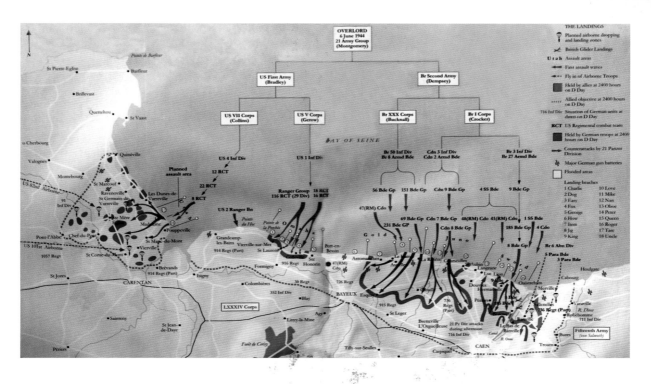

▲ Map showing the beaches and the paratroop and glider-borne landing zones.

➤ Paratrooper of the 101st 'Screaming Eagles' Airborne Division at the doorway of a C-47 carrying a rifle and M1A1 Bazooka. (US Army)

of the pathfinders shortly after midnight. The last of the airborne forces was dropped at 0404hrs and were resupplied by 408 tugs pulling 408 CG-4A and Horsa gliders. In all, 13,215 troops were dropped, with 223 artillery pieces and 1,641,448lb of combat equipment and supplies. Gliders delivered 4,047 troops, 110 artillery pieces, 281 jeeps

Did You Know?

Should D-Day have failed, General Dwight D. Eisenhower had prepared a speech in secret on 5 June, taking all the blame. He put it in his pocket in case it was needed. Six weeks later he found it again, still in his pocket.

and 412,477lb of combat equipment and supplies to their zones. Out of 805 C-47 'Skytrain' aircraft, only twenty were lost but, confused by the cloud and thrown off their course in evading the flak, some pilots flew high and fast and spilled their troops out of weaving aircraft. By dawn only 1,100 of Taylor's parachutists had reached their

Did You Know?
More than 130,000 men, 8,900 vehicles and 1,900 tons of stores were landed from the sea, and over 20,000 men from the air, in the first twenty-four hours, at a cost of over 6,000 American casualties.

rendezvous and, twenty-four hours later, he had collected fewer than 3,000.

The 82nd Division, commanded by Major General Matthew B. Ridgway, fared better and three-quarters of his paratroopers landed within 3 miles (5km) of the drop zone (DZ). They rallied quickly and formed smaller improvised squads, and two and

▲ 82nd and 101st Airborne Division badges. (Author)

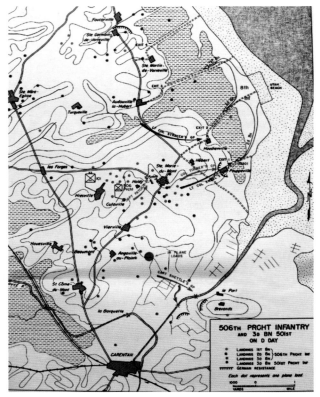

506TH PRCHT INFANTRY
AND 3D BN 501ST
ON D DAY

a half hours after the main drop they had taken Ste-Mère-Église, thus blocking the Cherbourg–Carentan road. But only twenty-two out of fifty-two gliders carrying guns, transport and signals equipment managed to find the landing zone (LZ) and the enemy forestalled the airborne attempt to seize the bridges over the Merderet, splitting the division along the line of an almost impassable belt of river and swamp.

By 1300hrs the 101st Division had linked up with the US 4th Infantry Division

◀ Geographically, Utah Beach, between Exits 2 and 3, was the first section of French soil to be occupied by Americans landing from the English Channel. 'Kilometer 00' marks the beginning of the 4th Division's and General Leclerc's 2nd Armoured Division's Liberty Highway, which runs both into Holland and across France to the German border.

▶ C-47A 42-100591 *Tico Belle* wearing the markings it wore on D-Day when it was one of ninety C-47As of the 436th Troop Carrier Group used in the lead formation of 177 transports carrying the 101st Airborne Division, 502nd Regiment and the 377th Parachute Artillery Battalion. (Author)

beach landings at Pouppeville, the most southerly exit off Utah Beach. By 1900hrs the Merderet crossing at Chef du Pont was controlled by 82nd Airborne Division. Elsewhere, paratroopers were so heavily engaged that they had no chance of blowing the bridges over the Douve or forming a compact bridgehead over the Merderet. The 101st Division's casualties totaled 1,240, of whom 182 were killed; the 82nd Division suffered 1,259 casualties, of whom 156 were killed. Of the 6,396 paratroopers of the 82nd who jumped, 272 were killed or injured as a result of the drop. Of the 6,600 paratroopers of the 101st Division, only about 2,500 had assembled by the end of the first day. By D-Day+6 the 82nd had secured the area north of Ste-Mère-Église after fierce fighting, and considerably delayed the German 243rd Infantry Division from contacting the Allied beach assault force.

The church at Ste-Mère-Église. (Author)

The only breaks in the 100ft-high cliffs running between Utah and Gold beaches were at Omaha Beach. The landings were, therefore, vital to connect the US troops at Utah Beach with the British and Canadian beaches to the east. There were fewer bunkers at Utah than at Omaha with the defences largely based on the flooded coastal plain behind the beaches. Omaha Beach was the objective of V Corps, commanded by Major General Leonard T. Gerow and comprised of the 29th and 1st US divisions. At Utah the objective of the 4th US Division of Major General Raymond O. Barton's VII Corps was to gain a beachhead, leading in time to the capture of the Cotentin Peninsula and of the port of Cherbourg.

As the heaviest landings at Omaha were to be made directly in front of the enemy strongpoints covering the natural exits off the 4-mile (6.5km) long beach instead of between them, Lieutenant General Omar Bradley, US First Army, on the USS *Augusta*, was relying on a heavy aerial and sea bombardment followed by a direct assault by troops to swamp the fortifications, which were believed to be undermanned. Before

Did You Know?

On 10 April 1944 Admiral Sir Bertram Ramsay, Naval Commander-in-Chief responsible for Operation Neptune, issued orders for the naval involvement on D-Day in a document that stretched to 1,100 pages. Ramsay later declared Neptune 'the greatest amphibious operation in history'.

➤➤ 1st Infantry Division at Weymouth prior to going to Omaha Beach. (USNA)

Did You Know?
On 2 May a British staff officer doing the *Daily Telegraph* crossword worked out that seventeen across – 'A US state' – was 'Utah'. On 22 May 'Omaha' appeared and then came 'Overlord' on 27 May, 'Mulberry' on 30 May and 'Neptune' on 1 June. MI5 investigated the compiler, Leatherhead schoolmaster Leonard Dawe, and put it down to a coincidence. However, forty years later it was revealed that the schoolmaster would get his pupils to fill out blank crosswords and then concocted clues to fit. These pupils spent some of their afternoons at American and Canadian camps nearby where they heard the soldiers using the code words!

➤ Two of the pictures taken by war photographer Robert Capa in the first wave on Omaha Beach. The pictures are grainy and some are a little blurred, but there is no doubt that they captured the hour of the attack.

dawn at 0555hrs, B-24 Liberator bombers hit Omaha Beach. This was followed by a naval bombardment by US Navy, Royal Navy and French battleships, and eleven destroyers provided close range support. At Utah the pre-landing shore bombardment started earlier than scheduled, at 0536hrs, because German gun batteries had already

◀ The lone GI struggling in the water is Ed Regen.

▲ Robert Capa, born Endre Friedman in Budapest on 22 October 1913, photographed five wars, including the Spanish Civil War and French Indo-China in the early 1950s. He was 41 years old in 1954 when he stepped on a land mine at Thai Binh, after taking pictures of French combat troops. He died a short time later. His epitaph: 'If the picture isn't good enough, you're not close enough.'

begun firing at the Allied ships. For fifty minutes following H-Hour the ships of the Task Force provided abundant and accurate naval gunfire support, especially on the remote and large-calibre batteries inaccessible to the ground troops.

From the outset everything went wrong at Omaha. USS *Texas* and other gunfire

➤ 'The End of Mulberry 'A" by Dwight C. Shepler. During 19–22 June the worst June storm for forty years wrought five times the amount of damage caused by enemy bombardment after D-Day. Many landing craft and DUKWs were lost and a total of 800 were driven ashore. American 'Mulberry A' off Ste-Laurent was wrecked and its parts used to repair the more carefully laid British port at Arromanches off Gold Beach, which was gravely damaged. It was to last another ten months, landing 2.5 million men, 500,000 vehicles and 4 million tons of supplies. (USN Combat Art Collection)

support ships pounded the beach exit leading to Vierville, but low cloud, bad visibility, smoke and dust made further identification of targets difficult. Rocket ships opened fire at extreme range and most fell short among the landing craft. The weather combined with the smoke and dust also hampered aerial bombardment

◄ C-47 glider tugs of the 442nd Troop Carrier Group and Horsa gliders at RAF Fulbeck in Lincolnshire. Paratroops carried by the group were dropped from forty-five aircraft at Ste-Mère-Église on D-Day, and fifty-six resupply sorties were flown the next day. (Author)

and bomb release was delayed to avoid hitting US troops, so most of the tonnage dropped by 484 B-24 Liberators landed 3 miles (5km) inland. Then the Task Force 'O' Commander, Rear Admiral John L. Hall Jr, concerned about fire from coastal batteries, began lowering assault craft 12 miles (19km) offshore. (The British were

Did You Know?

'Juno' was originally named 'Jelly' but changed to Juno by Churchill. Omaha and Utah were supposedly named after the respective birthplaces of the US V and VII Corps' commanders, General Leonard T. 'Gee' Gerow and Major General Lawton L. Collins. However, 'Lightning Joe' Collins was from Louisiana and Gerow from Virginia. Also, a little-known sixth beach, codenamed 'Band', to the east of the Orne River was reserved for use if a disaster occurred on any of the other beaches.

◄ HMS *Glasgow* pounding the Les Moulins area with the 8in cruiser USS *Quincy* in the background. At H-Hour on D-Day, *Quincy* opened up on the Crisbecq battery. The battery returned fire on the USS *Nevada*, which then turned her guns on the battery too. (IWM)

Did You Know?

'Rommel's Asparagus' was so called because his sketches of his obstacles made the beaches look like vegetable gardens. Rommel also ordered that the low-lying areas behind the coast be flooded to turn them into inaccessible marshland.

➤ A GMC DUKW amphibious truck on display at the Land Warfare Museum, IWM Duxford. (Author)

➤➤ American jeeps on board a landing craft. (USNA)

lowered less than 8 miles (13km) from shore.) Leading assault craft had to start their run-in while it was still dark. Twenty- seven DD (Duplex Drive, amphibious) tanks sank in 100ft of water and thirty-three men drowned. Three tanks were trapped by the

Did You Know?
American casualties at Omaha Beach were the highest of all the beaches, and the greatest in one battle since the Battle of Antietam Creek in the American Civil War on 17 September 1862 when the bloodiest day in American history resulted in 22,719 casualties; 12,401 to the Army of the Potomac and 10,318 to General Lee's Confederate forces.

jamming of the ramp of the landing craft and were carried in. Two made the shore. The thirty-two DD tanks of the 743rd Tank Battalion were not launched because of the rough sea and were taken all the way to the beach in their eight landing craft.

The first landing craft carrying the 116th Infantry Regiment of the 29th

◄ Rangers aboard their landing craft.
(US Army)

Did You Know?

One of the battalions in the German 716th Division comprised *Osttruppen* – Polish, Czech and Russian volunteers. Their officers and non-commissioned officers were German, but the German troops they commanded were not fully committed to the cause.

Division and the 16th Infantry of the experienced 1st Division – the 'Big Red One' – set off at 0520hrs. Fifteen minutes later, two companies of the 741st Tank Battalion destined for the eastern half of Omaha began launching their thirty-two DD Sherman tanks 6,000yd

Did You Know?

Robert Capa, having been with the 1st Infantry Division in Sicily, went ashore with the first wave on Omaha rather than go in with Regimental HQ after the first waves of infantry. On D+1 his ten rolls of film arrived at *Life* magazine in London for developing but the 16-year-old darkroom assistant inadvertently melted the negatives and only eleven frames were salvageable. They were published in *Life* magazine on 19 June.

▲ British LCA 1377 carrying Rangers from Weymouth heading for the shore. (US Navy)

(5,400m) from the shore. (They should have been launched from about 2 miles (3.2km) offshore so that faster LCI and LCA transport would not reach the shore before them and be deprived of immediate armoured support.) At least ten Landing Craft (Vehicle, Personnel) (LCVP) ('Higgins boats') that were top-heavy with guns, ammunition, sandbags and men on board were lost when they were swamped or rolled over in the sea during the run-in. Waves swamped eleven of the thirteen

➤ LST 134 and other LSTs of Task Force O at Portland Harbour on 5 June.

Did You Know?

General Dwight D. Eisenhower (1890–1969) put himself in for the entrance examination for West Point and passed top of his class. During the Second World War he was never sent overseas and never saw battle. In June 1942 he was promoted over 366 senior officers to be commander of US troops in Europe and he commanded the Allied 'Torch' landings in North Africa. After the war, 'Ike' ran for the US presidency and served two terms in the White House (1953–61).

◀ LST 314 berthed at Portland Harbour.

DUKW amphibious trucks carrying the 105mm howitzers, most of them when still circling in the rendezvous area. Only six of the sixteen armoured bulldozers reached shore and three were immediately destroyed. Less than half the companies in assault battalions were landed within 800yd (730m) of their sectors.

In the first wave 1,450 men of the 1st Infantry Division in thirty-six landing craft

◄ M4 Sherman medium tanks on LCT 210 with hooded structures on the rear of the tanks' decks to allow air to enter the engine and the exhaust fumes to escape without seawater flooding it and 'drowning' the tank's engine. (USNA)

Did You Know?

For his actions and inspiration, Private Carlton Barrett of the reconnaissance platoon of HQ Company 18th/1st Infantry was one of three men on the Omaha landings who were awarded the Medal of Honor. He waded ashore in neck-deep waves and then returned under fire to rescue floundering comrades who were close to drowning. Ashore during the day, he worked as a guide, a runner and assisted the wounded.

◀ 'Mulberry At Work' by Dwight C. Shepler. (USN Combat Art Collection)

headed for the beaches in heavy seas. The lightly armed infantrymen stormed ashore and suffered terrible losses as they were pinned down on the beach by the German 352nd Field Regiment. The attackers had to make frontal assaults on pillboxes and strongpoints without sufficient DD tanks and heavy bulldozing equipment, and it took some companies forty-five minutes to reach the cover of the sea wall. By 0700hrs the situation was chaotic, as troops were pinned down and forced to take cover behind mined beach defences. Engineers were unable to clear obstacles and 40 per cent of the 270 specially trained demolition men were killed or wounded. Thirty LCT transports waiting offshore could not come in because of shelling. The second wave of troops added to the confusion and over-crowding on Omaha, and the congestion became so great that the head Beachmaster ordered that no more boats were to land until it was cleared. Two companies of 2nd Rangers in the first wave, coming in on the edge of an area codenamed 'Dog Green', did manage to reach the sea wall but at the cost of half their strength. On the most easterly beach, 'Fox Green', elements of five different companies became entangled and the situation was little improved by the equally disorganised landings of the second wave. Two more companies of one battalion joined the melee and, having drifted east in the first wave, finally made their traumatic landing on Fox Green: two of their six boats were swamped on their detour to the east and, as they came in under fire, three of the four remaining boats were damaged by artillery or mines and the fourth became trapped on an obstacle.

The situation on Omaha was now on the verge of catastrophe. In the absence of clear reports, Lieutenant General Omar

Bradley ordered Major Chester 'Chet' Hansen to the beach in a landing craft, 11 miles (18km) away, to get a first-hand situation report. Another staff officer reported landing craft milling around 'like a stampeded herd of cattle'. Hansen returned to the USS *Augusta* to report to Bradley that 'Disaster lay ahead'. From 0810hrs some of

Did You Know?

Two other Medal of Honor recipients of the Normandy campaign are buried at Omaha: Tech Sergeant Frank Peregory of the 116th Infantry Division, for his meritorious action at Grandcamp Maisy on 8 June; and 1st Lieutenant Jimmie W. Monteith Jr of the 16th Infantry, 1st Division, whose act of conspicuous gallantry took place on 6 June on Omaha.

the destroyers began to break the ceasefire order that suspended naval gunfire support at 0630hrs and the attack up the cliffs began, assisted by tanks and destroyers firing from close inshore. At 0950hrs Rear Admiral Carleton F. Bryant, Naval Gunfire Support Group 'O', ordered his seventeen warships to move in closer. Employing pairs of Spitfires to spot targets from the air, due to the absence of any surviving fire control officers, at least eight destroyers – some as close as 800yd (730m) from the beach – opened up on inland strongpoints and gun batteries. In desperation Eisenhower had issued an order to the Allied Air Forces to bomb Omaha Beach, but the order could not be carried out, which was fortunate because the battle had turned and the German defences had already been penetrated in four places.

'C' Company of the 116th Regiment led the charge off of 'Dog White' by forcing gaps in the wire with a Bangalore torpedo and wire cutters, and the 5th Rangers joined the advance and created more openings. The command party established themselves at the top of the bluff and other elements of the 116th joined them, having earlier moved laterally along the beach. Other units of the 16th and 116th came together and climbed the bluffs at 'Easy Red'. The beaches were still under heavy fire but once on top of the bluffs overlooking Omaha, troops moved laterally to attack enemy fortifications. A German counter-attack in the Colleville area in the early afternoon was stopped by 'firm American resistance' and heavy losses were reported. At 2000hrs the Americans captured Ste-Laurent and Colleville. Approaches to the beach exits were gradually cleared, with minefields lifted and holes blown in the embankment to permit the passage of vehicles. As the tide receded, engineers were also able to resume their work of clearing the beach obstacles and, by the end of the evening, thirteen gaps were open and marked.

US casualties were heavy but the Germans could not halt the attack and on the second tide of the day 25,000 more men and 4,000 vehicles were ashore.

It had been hoped that V Corps might have a beachhead 16 miles (26km) wide and 5–6 miles (8–9.5km) deep by nightfall, but only pockets of US forces covered an area about 5 miles (8km) wide while confused, hard-fought individual actions pushed the foothold out barely 1½ mile (2.5km) deep in the Colleville area to the east, even less to the west of Ste-Laurent and an isolated penetration in the Vierville area. Pockets of enemy resistance still fought on behind the American frontline and the whole beachhead remained under artillery fire. Losses were appalling. Casualties for V Corps were estimated at 3,000 killed, wounded and missing, the heaviest casualties taken by the infantry, tanks and engineers in the first landings. The 16th and 116th Regimental Combat Teams (RCTs) lost about 1,000 men each; the 29th Division had suffered 2,440 casualties; and the 1st Division lost 1,744, with most of these in the first two hours. One of the reasons for the high losses was the shortage of heavy weapons and artillery, as only 100 tons of the 2,400 tons of supplies scheduled for D-Day were actually landed. The German 352nd Division suffered 1,200 killed, wounded and missing (about 20 per cent of its strength) and 2,500 more taken prisoner. At midnight General Dietrich Kraiss, commander of the 352nd Division, advised that he had sufficient forces to contain the Americans on D+1 but that he would need reinforcements thereafter. He was told that there were no more reserves available.

Compared to Omaha, the assault on Utah Beach was almost a textbook landing. By midnight 23,250 troops were ashore and casualties were light. Losses to the 4th Infantry Division were 197 killed and 60 missing, presumed drowned. The air bombardment, too, was more effective than at Omaha, with 276 B-26 Marauder aircraft destroying Blockhouse 5 and all five artillery pieces. But, as at Omaha, it could all have gone so wrong. At the outset the guiding craft for the landing force was sunk and the remaining ships headed off course. Though a strong current carried the 4th Infantry Division 2,000yd (1,820m) south of their intended target, the beach was less heavily defended than the one originally designated for the attack.

The landing on the 3 miles (5km) of Utah Beach had been planned in four waves. The first consisted of twenty Higgins boats, each carrying a thirty-man assault team from the 8th Infantry Regiment. Ten craft were to land on 'Tare Green Beach', opposite the strongpoint at Les Dunes de Varreville. The other ten were intended for 'Uncle Red Beach', 1,000yd (915m) further south. The entire operation was timed against the touchdown of this first assault wave, which was scheduled to take place at 0630hrs. Eight LCTs, each carrying four amphibious DD Tanks, were

Did You Know?

57-year-old Brigadier General Theodore Roosevelt Jr, son of the 26th US President 'Teddy' Roosevelt, a veteran of the First World War and three assault landings in the Second World War, went ashore in the first wave on Utah, carrying only a cane and a .45 calibre pistol. He set an example of coolness under fire and when he realised that the lead regiment had landed in the wrong place, said, 'We'll start the war right here'. His leadership earned him the award of the Medal of Honor.

scheduled to land at the same time. The second wave consisted of another thirty-two Higgins boats with additional troops of the two assault battalions, some combat engineers and also eight naval demolition teams that were to clear the beach of underwater obstacles. The third wave, timed for H+15 minutes, contained eight more Higgins boats with DD tanks. It was followed within two minutes by the fourth wave, mainly detachments of the 237th and 299th Combat Engineer Battalions, to clear the beaches between high- and low-water marks.

The first wave arrived at the line of departure on time and all twenty craft were dispatched abreast. Support craft to the rear fired machine-guns, primarily in the hope of exploding mines. When the LCVPs were 300–400yd (275–365m) from the beach, the assault company commanders fired special smoke projectors to signal the lifting of naval support fire. Almost exactly at H-Hour the assault craft lowered their ramps and 600 men waded through waist-deep water for the last 100yd (90m) to the beach. The actual touchdown on the beach was, therefore, a few minutes late, but the delay was negligible and had no effect on the phasing of the succeeding waves. Enemy artillery fired a few air bursts at the incoming craft, but otherwise there was no opposition at H-Hour. The first troops to reach shore were from the 2nd Battalion of the 8th Infantry Regiment, with the 1st Battalion landing a few minutes later. Both came ashore considerably south of the designated beaches. The 2nd Battalion should have hit Uncle Red Beach opposite 'Exit 3', and the 1st Battalion was supposed to land directly opposite the strongpoint at Les Dunes de Varreville. The landings, however, were made astride 'Exit 2' about 2,000yd (1,820m) south.

At 0631hrs, one minute behind schedule, the first wave of up to twenty Higgins boats, each with a thirty-man assault team from the 8th Infantry Regiment, 4th Infantry Division, came to within 100yd (90m) of the shore. Some twenty-eight of the thirty-two 33-ton amphibious DD Sherman tanks were landed. The 4th Infantry Division disembarked opposite Pouppeville instead of their objective at Ste-Martin-de-Varreville, 1½ miles (2.5km) to the north. Colonel Russell 'Red' Reeder decided that they should wade through the flooded fields behind the beach towards their objective. With water up to their waists, and sometimes over their heads, they struggled on while the causeways and fields came under fire from the battery at Ste-Marcouf. At 0640hrs almost all the DD tanks had been landed successfully and the small pockets of enemy opposition were quickly dealt with.

The beach defences were mostly cleared by high tide. By 0730hrs all resistance from the German 709th Division had ended. At 0800hrs Brigadier Theodore Roosevelt ordered in follow-up troops, and by 0930hrs Exits 1, 2 and 3 were secured. At 1000hrs six battalions

▲ '... Wood timbers/ cross ties and barbed wire were attached to mines. I saw a couple of dead men draped over these obstacles in the shallow water...' ('Low Tide' by Mitchell Jamieson) (USN Combat Art Collection)

65

landed, including follow-up troops – 12th and 22nd RCTs. The La Madeleine battery and the beach exits were captured and twenty-six assault waves were landed before noon. At 1300hrs the 101st Airborne Division and the 4th Infantry Division linked up at Pouppeville, which provided a route and the extra forces with which to attack and capture Ste-Marie-du-Mont later in the day. US troops gradually fanned out to Beuzeville au Plain and Les Forges. By 1800hrs 21,328 men and 1,700 vehicles were ashore, and, by midnight, the troops had reached about 6 miles (9.5km) inland.

The landings left permanent mental and physical scars on those who took part and, for most, the nightmares have never left them. One veteran of Omaha described the experience thus:

When you run over unconscious men, or men lying on their bellies, it's tough to keep your balance. There is no room. You go into the water, but the water is washing bodies in and out. Everywhere there are body pieces – a testicle here, a head there, an ass here. Crap all over the place. Intestines, intestines, intestines. That's what Omaha beach was.

Allied intelligence had pinpointed seventy-three fixed coastal gun batteries that could menace the invasion. At Pointe-du-Hoc, a cliff rising 100ft (30m) high from a very rocky beach, 3.7 miles (6km) west of Vierville, a six-gun battery (thought to be 155mm calibre, with a range of 25,000yd (22.8km)) could engage ships at sea and fire directly onto Utah and Omaha. In addition to the main concrete emplacements, many of which were connected by tunnels or protected walkways, there were trenches and machine-gun posts constructed around the perimeter fences and the cliff edge. The garrison numbered about 200 men of the static 716th Coastal Defence Division, mostly made up of elderly Germans or conscripts from German-occupied territories. In anticipation of landings by Allied commandos, 240mm

◄ A grinning US Ranger holding a 60mm Bazooka anti-tank rocket launcher, which could also be used against bunkers and fortifications. (USNA)

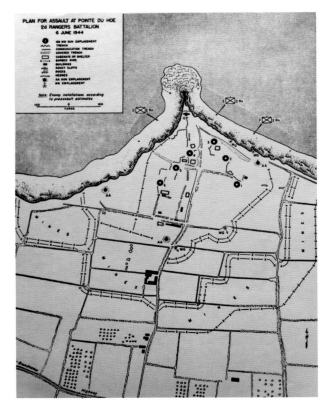

Did You Know?

The 2.36in Rocket Launcher M1A1 or the later two-piece M9, based on a pre-war, shoulder-fired recoilless weapon, was commonly known among US troops as the 'Bazooka' after the wind instrument played by Bob Burns, an American comedian in the 1940s.

shells were attached to trip wires and placed at 100yd (90m) intervals along the cliff. The gun positions were bombed throughout May, with heavier attacks both day and night during the three days before D-Day, and then again during the night of 5 June. Then, at 0630hrs three companies (225 men) of the 2nd Ranger Battalion, using rocket-propelled grapple hooks attached to climbing ropes and portable extension ladders, scaled the cliffs within ten minutes after landing and captured the position. The assault was led by Lieutenant Colonel James Earl Rudder, a 34-year-old college teacher and football coach from Brady, Texas.

◄◄ Plan for assault on Pointe-du-Hoc (note the misspelt 'Hoe') by the 2nd Ranger Battalion. It was believed that the Germans had a battery of six 155mm guns at the top of this rocky promontory, from where they could dominate Utah and Omaha beaches.

◄ Pointe-du-Hoc was taken by three companies of US Rangers on D-Day. They would later have to hold out against German attacks until 8 June, when they were finally relieved by the advance of US troops from Omaha Beach. (Author)

▲ 2nd Ranger Battalion marching along the seafront at Weymouth. (USNA)

Did You Know?

On 5/6 June, in Operations 'Taxable' and 'Glimmer', 'Phantom Fleets' were created on enemy radar screens by RAF bombers and eighteen Royal Navy small vessels towed 'Filbert' balloons containing a special reflecting device to make the Germans believe that an invasion force was attacking the French coast between Dieppe and Cap d'Antifer. Twenty-nine RAF four-engine bombers carrying eighty-two radio jammers obliterated the German night-fighter frequencies for more than five hours, and a 'Mandrel' jamming screen rendered useless all but 5 per cent of the *Freya* radars between Cherbourg and Le Havre.

Meanwhile C Company, 2nd Ranger Battalion was to scale the bluffs of Pointe-de-la-Percée, 1¼ mile (2km) north-west of Vierville. Lieutenant Colonel Maxwell Schneider's 5th Ranger Battalion and the 2nd Battalion's A and B Companies constituted Task Force 'C', reinforcements which were to wait offshore. If Schneider did not receive a signal by H+30 he was to land his men on Omaha Beach and proceed overland through Pointe-de-la-Percée to attack Pointe-du-Hoc. (Schneider's men were not called upon so they moved 4 miles (6.5km) east to 'Dog White', where they spearheaded the advance off Omaha Beach and had captured Vierville by evening.)

The fortifications at Pointe-du-Hoc came under heavy fire from H-40 minutes to H-5 minutes from 10 miles (16km) offshore by the USS *Texas*, which fired about 250 14in shells at the six-gun battery at Pointe-du-Hoc before changing targets to fire another 350 shells at the resistance nests at Omaha. Then eighteen medium bombers carried

➤ The 2nd Ranger Battalion in British-manned LCAs and LSIs at Weymouth. (USNA)

out a last-minute strike on the German positions just before the Rangers were due to arrive. But when the sea bombardment had been lifted according to schedule, and as the Rangers were landed, the Germans filtered back into the fortifications and were waiting for them with machine-guns, rifles and hand-grenades, which they rolled

◄ The remains of a steel-reinforced bunker near the clifftop give a dramatic demonstration of the effects of the bombardment. The USS *Texas* saturated the Pointe with fire from its ten 14in guns prior to the Rangers' landing. (Author)

down the cliffs. At 0708hrs the 2nd Ranger Battalion landed and began scaling the cliffs which led to the battery, but they arrived forty minutes later than scheduled and from a direction parallel with the coast, having been misdirected to Pointe-de-la-Percée nearby, which allowed the battery garrison to spot them and open fire with small arms and 20mm flak. Up until this point the 2nd Ranger's casualties numbered thirty to forty, but later that day the German 1st Battalion, 914th Regiment began a series of counter-attacks that nearly wiped out the small bridgehead and caused more casualties.

The Rangers discovered to their dismay that the big guns were not in place on the cliffs but that five of the six guns were well camouflaged and unguarded in an orchard 2½ miles (4km) further inland. (The sixth gun had been damaged by bombing and had been removed elsewhere for repair.) Telephone poles had been put in their place in the pillbox to deceive the Allied reconnaissance. The 2nd Rangers proceeded to destroy the firing mechanisms of the guns and stop their murderous barrage from raining down on Omaha and Utah.

That night the 2nd Rangers were driven into a small enclave along the cliff, barely 200 yards wide, but they held out until noon on 8 June, helped by fire from destroyers, when they were relieved by Lieutenant Colonel Schneider's men. By then 2nd Ranger casualties were 135 killed, wounded and missing – a casualty rate of 60 per cent. C Company, 2nd Ranger Battalion suffered 50 per cent casualties (thirty-eight out of sixty-four men) clearing the German positions at Pointe-de-la-Percée before proceeding overland to Pointe-du-Hoc.

The 6th Airborne Division's task on the eve of D-Day was to support Sir Miles Dempsey's British Second Army and Henry Crerar's First Canadian Army by seizing and holding the left flank of the bridgehead. The 5th Parachute Brigade was to take the ground each side of the bridges over the Canal du Caen at Bénouville and the River Orne at Ranville, and on the same day seize and hold positions on the long wooded ridge beyond the waterways, running from Troarn in the south to the sea. This ridge, with the bridges behind, would eventually form the critical left flank of the invasion force and the bridges had to be kept intact to permit Allied troops and supplies to pass easily to and fro. Major John Howard commanded the glider-borne *coup de main* party of six platoons (150 men) of D Company, 2nd Battalion, Oxfordshire and Buckinghamshire Light Infantry, and thirty men of 249 Field Company (Airborne) Royal Engineers for the capture of the bridges. After capture their task was to hold the bridges until relieved. Brigadier James Hill's 3rd Parachute Brigade, made up of the

Did You Know?
RAF bombers, giving the impression of a much larger force, dropped 500 dummy parachutists called 'Ruperts' equipped with sound and light simulators to mimic a small arms battle, relieving some pressure on US airborne forces around Ste-Mère-Église when the 915th Regiment abandoned Omaha Beach and wasted several precious hours trying to intercept the dummies.

> Piper Bill Millin, who piped Lord Lovat's commandos across Pegasus Bridge. The only 'weapon' he carried was his set of pipes. He wore a battle dress tunic over his Cameron-clan kilt and a green commando beret. He also carried a standard heavy Bergen rucksack with his rations and personal equipment.

8th and 9th Battalions and the 1st Canadian Parachute Battalion (1,800 men), was to prevent enemy reinforcements moving towards the British beachhead. The 8th Battalion and the 1st Canadian Brigade were to destroy five bridges in the flooded valley of the Dives.

A 750-strong assault force in the 9th Battalion, commanded by Lieutenant Colonel Terence B.H. Otway DSO, was

◄ Churchill AVRE displayed at Pegasus Bridge.

◀◀ A Horsa, used as a troop-carrying glider.

◀ Major John Howard's bust at Pegasus Bridge. (Author)

Did You Know?

Ten warships of the Royal Norwegian Navy in exile, forty-three ships of the Norwegian Merchant Navy and three fighter squadrons – 66, 331 and 332, 132 Wing, Second Tactical Air Force – flying Spitfire IXs, took part in D-Day. A total of 800 Danes also served, mostly aboard ships.

to silence a battery of four concrete gun emplacements on high ground near the village of Merville, 3 miles (5km) east of Ouistreham. Intelligence indicated that the battery contained four 155mm guns, each capable of bombarding the landing beaches, and 160 men in fifteen to twenty weapon pits, each with four to five machine-guns and, possibly, three 20mm anti-aircraft guns. The guns were in four concrete emplacements built with reinforced concrete walls 6ft (1.8m) thick,

Did You Know?

By June 1944 more than one-third of New Zealand's overseas manpower – about 35,000 men – were serving in Britain. Of these, about 30,000 were in the RAF or in the six RNZAF squadrons and they took part in every phase of Operation Overlord. Virtually all of the 11,000 Australian aircrew also participated.

British paras aboard their Horsa glider look tense as they await take-off.

two of which were also covered by 12ft (3.6m) of earth, and secured with steel doors. They were in a fenced area of 700 x 500yd (640 x 450m), within which a belt of barbed wire, double in places, 15ft (4.5m) thick and 5ft (1.5m) high protected the perimeter. A 400yd (365m) anti-tank ditch, 15ft (4.5m) wide by 10ft (3m) deep around

Did You Know?

More than 10,000 aircraft were involved in the invasion. By midnight on 5 June, 1,333 heavy RAF bombers dropped 5,316 tons of bombs on radar stations and the ten most important German gun batteries in the assault area. In the twenty-four hours between the night of 5 and 6 June, the RAF dropped 15,000 and 20,000 tons of bombs. The Allies flew 14,674 sorties on D-Day, including: 2,656 by Eighth Bomber Command; 3,587 by Ninth Air Force; 2,249 by Second Tactical Air Force; and 912 by Air Defence of Great Britain (ADGB). RAF Coastal Command flew 353 anti-U-boat and ship patrols without loss. Allied losses from 2100hrs on 5 June to sunrise on 7 June were 131 aircraft. In comparison, the Luftwaffe only flew 319 sorties.

◀ Advertisement urging civilians to buy War Saving bonds.

two sides, was incomplete but mines had been sown profusely, and there was a dual-purpose gun position and about fifteen weapon pits. Outside the main position was a wired-in strongpoint with five machine-gun emplacements and several other anti-aircraft gun positions. The 9th Battalion rehearsed the attack on a full-size mock-up

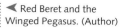

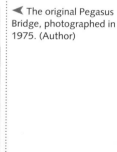

▲ Headgear worn by Lord Lovat's Scouts.

of the battery, built specially at a farm at West Woodhay, near Newbury.

On the night of 5/6 June at 5,000ft (1.5km) over Cabourg the gliders carrying the *coup de main* party were released from their tugs and they began their 5-mile (8km) glide to the bridges over the Canal de Caen and River Orne. Incredibly, three of the gliders landed within 30yd (27m) of the Canal de Caen Bridge. By 0035hrs the Canal de Caen Bridge (subsequently renamed 'Pegasus Bridge') was in British hands at a cost of two men killed and fourteen wounded. Two other gliders landed near the bridge over the River Orne (subsequently renamed 'Horsa Bridge'), which was undefended. A sixth glider landed 7 miles (11km) away near the River Dives. Spitfires flew over at about 10,000ft (3km) and Major Howard signalled that they had captured the bridge, although he would have to beat off counter-attacks from German tanks and artillery for more than twelve hours. As the Germans moved to counter-attack at 0050hrs, 2,000 men of the 5th Parachute Brigade and 400 containers were dropped north of Ranville by 110 RAF aircraft, and its 7th Battalion moved to reinforce the defensive positions around the bridges. At 1330hrs Brigadier Lord Lovat's 1st Special Service Brigade composed of four Army and one Royal Marines Commando unit, reached Pegasus Bridge en route to help other units of the Airborne Division. At 1500hrs the 7th Battalion occupied Bénouville and Le Port, the villages closest to the bridges, and continued to hold them against repeated

counter-attacks by the German 21st Panzer Division.

Meanwhile, plans to attack the Merville battery had gone awry. Low cloud obscured the battery and a bombing attack by 93 out of 104 Halifaxes and Lancasters at 0025hrs resulted in nearly all the 4,000lb of

▲ Wartime map of the Merville Battery and surrounding area.

bombs dropped missing the target. Almost all of the 9th Battalion and much of the brigade was scattered over a wide area, many landing in the flooded fields, and only about 150 paratroopers were grouped together for the march on the objective. No support could be expected from the glider-borne troops, as all three Horsa gliders had been lost and landed several miles from the battery. Colonel Otway, however,

➤ The bust of Lieutenant Colonel Terence B.H. Otway DSO. (Author)

➤➤ Richard Todd, the star of many post-war film epics such as *The Dam Busters*, *Yangtse Incident* and *The Longest Day*, was a 23-year-old 1st Lieutenant in the 7th Light Infantry Battalion, 5th Parachute Brigade. From a total of five officers and 120 men originally in A Company, there were no surviving officers and fewer than twenty men by the middle of 6 June. (Author)

was determined to take the battery with what forces he had left. He reorganised his men into seven parties: two to breach the main wire; four to deal with the four guns; and one to make a diversion at the main entrance. Gaps were blown in the wire and the paratroopers stormed the battery. The diversion party attacked through the main gate and hand-to-hand fighting ensued for twenty minutes until the Germans finally capitulated. Twenty-two prisoners were taken and at 0445hrs the success signal was fired. (HMS *Arethusa* was standing by to pound the battery with her 6in guns at 0550hrs if the attack failed.) The seventy-five paratroopers still standing discovered four Czechoslovakian 10cm LFH14/19 field howitzers on wheels, which had a range of 4 miles (6.5km) and were made by Škoda, and these were also destroyed. Later in the day, the German 736th Grenadier Regiment reoccupied the battery and the guns opened fire. The next day Nos 4 and 5 Troops, 3 Commando assaulted the battery and the defenders were overcome, but the enemy counter-attacked using self-propelled artillery and drove the commandos out.

The British and Canadians were to land on Gold, Sword and Juno beaches in the eastern sector. XXX Corps' 50th British (Northumberland) Division, commanded by Major General Douglas Graham, was to land on Gold Beach and capture Bayeux and the Caen–Bayeux road, enabling the Allies to use the east–west road communications, and to join up with the American troops at Omaha Beach. At Juno

➤ Barnacle-encrusted caissons used in the Mulberry B Harbour on the seashore at Arromanches. (Author)

▲ Aerial view of Arromanches.

about 15,000 troops of the 3rd Canadian Division, commanded by Major General Rodney Keller, and attached British units were to advance inland and join up with Gold and Sword beaches on either side. At Sword Major General Thomas Rennie's 3rd British Division were to advance inland towards the city of Caen and link up with the airborne troops who had landed by parachute and glider and were protecting the eastern flank of landings against German counter-attack.

The pre-assault bombardment on all the British and Canadian beaches was twenty minutes longer than that on the American ones because half-tide, when the landings were scheduled, came later in the east. Between 0510 and 0725hrs the bombardment of Gold Beach was conducted by Task Force 'K', comprising the cruisers HMS *Orion*, *Ajax*, *Argonaut* and *Emerald*, the Dutch gunboat HMNS *Flares* and thirteen destroyers including the Polish ORP *Krakowiak*. Fifteen minutes before H-Hour (H-Hour was 0730hrs hours) Landing Craft (Rocket) (LCR) opened fire on the beaches with salvoes of 127mm rockets. 25-pounder Sexton self-propelled guns in landing craft also added to their fire. At H-7 minutes RAF bombers commenced their air attacks on the German defences, concentrating principally on the coastal batteries in the area. Five minutes later the USAAF arrived over the beachhead to combine their attacks with the shore bombardment. DD tanks were to be launched to swim ashore five minutes before H-Hour but, with a 15kt wind whipping waves up to 4ft and a strong tide, it was decided that the DD tanks would be landed directly on the beach. At 0725hrs the first units of 231st and 69th Brigades touched down. DD tanks and beach clearance groups, delayed by bad weather, were landed directly on

Did You Know?
Late on 4 June, two X-craft (midget submarines that had a crew of five and were battery powered with a diesel engine for recharging) took up station off Gold Beach to act as navigational markers pinpointing the landing positions of Task Force 'S' (for Sword) and Task Force 'J' (for Juno) using automatic radio beacons and telescopic masts fitted with powerful lights.

▲ Panoramic view of Arromanches and the remains of the Mulberry Harbour at low tide in 2004.

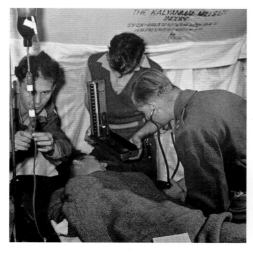

on the open beaches between the Dorset Regiment and the town of La Rivière. As with all the British beaches, success hinged on the speed with which tanks could be put ashore. The tanks of 8th Armoured Brigade were landed by the 15th LCT Flotilla under Lieutenant Commander Porteous. (They subsequently landed the 7th Armoured

to the beach thereafter. The 50th Infantry Division and 8th Armoured Brigade hit a defensive wall of 2,500 steel and concrete obstacles, covered by strong German troop emplacements, on a 3-mile (5km) stretch of coast and came under heavy artillery fire. At 0730hrs the Green Howards landed

Division and many hundreds of tanks and armoured vehicle reinforcements until the Mulberry harbours were fully operational.) At 0930hrs Les Roquettes was captured, but at 0950hrs there was stiff resistance at Le Hamel and the Commandos headed for Port-en-Bessin to link up with the American forces there. By mid-morning, landings of the follow-up assault units brought the 7th Armoured Division – the famous 'Desert Rats' – ashore and at 1050hrs the reserve brigades began to land, seven beach exits having been secured.

Of the six regiments on Sword, Juno and Gold which had been designated DD tanks for the assault, the weather was considered too rough to launch. However, this was not communicated to two of the regiments on Sword – the Nottinghamshire (Sherwood Rangers) Yeomanry, which launched from 1,000yd (915m) out, and the 13th/18th Royal Hussars, which launched from

Did You Know?

Up to twenty-five Australian officers who had experience of amphibious landings in New Guinea were seconded to the British Army to assist in the training of amphibious troops. No members of the Australian Army died in D-Day operations.

4,000yd (3.6km) out. The remainder were landed dry on the beaches and caused some delay in supporting the infantry regiments. Four of the first five flail tanks onto the beach at Le Hamel were knocked out, burned furiously and bulbous black clouds of smoke enveloped the leading troops and obscured the beach. At 0745hrs troops

◀◀ A caisson at Arromanches with the cliffs in the background. (Author)

made slow progress against raking fire, but three of the Sword Beach exits were cleared within the hour. C and D Companies, Royal Hampshires, having reached the sea wall east of Le Hamel, exploited a gap in the coastal wire and minefield belt and pushed inland in depth, outflanking and capturing Asnelles. By 0800hrs this movement was under way and, from 0820–0825hrs, follow-up battalions and 47 Royal Marine Commando landed between the 2nd Battalion, the Dorsets and Hampshires. With the tide rising, three of the Commandos' landing craft foundered on underwater obstacles and caused the loss of forty-three men.

At Juno Beach local naval commanders delayed H-Hour from 0735hrs to 0745hrs until the tide was so high that landing craft could clear the treacherous offshore reefs. However, delayed by a choppy sea, the leading assault craft headed in almost thirty minutes later than scheduled and were borne by the tide for several hundred yards through the belt of heavily mined obstacles. Twenty of the leading twenty-four landing craft were lost or damaged, and only six of the forty Centaur tanks mounting 95mm howitzers and manned by Royal Marines made the shore. At 0750hrs the Canadian 7th Brigade, the Royal Winnipeg Regiment and the Regina Rifles were first ashore on the right flank of Juno, west of the River Seulles, followed minutes later, opposite a strongpoint in the village of Bernières, by the Canadian 8th Brigade and eight to ten DD tanks manned by the Canadian 1st Hussars. On the left, ahead of the armour and running the gauntlet to the sea wall, were the Queen's Own Regiment of Canada, the North Shores and the Canadian 8th Brigade. Losses were significant but the survivors moved quickly and were already involved in heavy fighting at Courseulles,

◄◄ This view, at low tide at Arromanches, gives some idea of the distance that men had to storm ashore on D-Day under withering machine-gun fire.

➤ Canadian soldiers land from LCTs on Juno in the afternoon of 6 June. (NAC)

North Nova Scotia Highlanders going ashore from the HQ ship *Hilary* in LCI 299 at Bernières-sur-Mer. *Hilary* (the former British (Booth) liner, which after conversion could carry six landing craft), arrived at Juno at 0558hrs on 6 June as part of Assault Convoy J11. Though suffering slight damage in a bomb near-miss at 0410hrs on 13 June, *Hilary* became the flagship of the Eastern Task Force on 24 June. (RCN)

Bernières-sur-Mer and Ste-Aubin-sur-Mer as the delayed DDs struggled ashore.

At 0830hrs 48 Royal Marine Commando landed at Ste-Aubin and headed east. Little beach clearance took place due to the high tide and rough seas and the beaches became congested and were under heavy fire. By 0930hrs flail tanks opened

Did You Know?

Company Sergeant Major Stan Hollis, 6th Battalion, Green Howards, was the only man to win the Victoria Cross on D-Day. Hollis died in 1972. When his widow sold his VC at auction it fetched £32,000, a record at the time for this most distinguished decoration.

100

The vast array of ships off Sword Beach from German positions across the River Orne.

British ships at the Mulberry B Harbour at Arromanches with surrounding 'Gooseberry' sections (a ring of sunken merchant ships towed from Scotland and sunk alongside the Mulberry sections to act as breakwaters). The MoWT (Ministry of War Transport) *Empire Perdita* is in the middle to the left. (IWM)

exits on both sides of the River Seulles and the worst of the craters had been bridged by fascines and bridging tanks. From 0930hrs onwards, 8th Brigade took Bernières-sur-Mer as heavy enemy gunfire was in progress. By 1040hrs five beach

▲ CSM Stan Hollis VC. (IWM)

Did You Know?

The only Luftwaffe presence over the invasion beaches on 6 June were two Focke Wulf FW190s flown by *Oberstleutnant* Josef 'Pips' Priller and his wingman, Heinz Wodarczyk, who each made a full-throttle (400mph) low-level (50ft) strafing run over Sword Beach with cannons and machine-guns before landing nearby at Creil.

Did You Know?

As night fell on D-Day, all five beachheads were established along a 50-mile (80km) front and almost 155,000 Allied troops were positioned across nearly 80 square miles (130 square km) of France: 55,000 Americans plus 15,500 who had parachuted or glided across the Channel and 75,215 British and Canadian went ashore on D-Day. In the first six days over 300,000 men, 54,000 vehicles and 104,000 tons of stores were unloaded.

➤ Front page of the *Daily Mirror* on Wednesday 7 June.

▲ Sherman Duplex Drive (DD) tank displayed on Juno Beach in 1974. (Author)

exits had been cleared. At 1112hrs, after heavy fighting, 7th Brigade secured the beach exit at Courseulles, but the arrival of the Canadian 9th Brigade caused further congestion. At 1115hrs Ste-Aubin-sur-Mer fell to the Canadians and at 1120hrs Taillerville, Banville and Ste Croix were captured.

Did You Know?
One out of every eleven Americans who took part in the cross-Channel invasion on D-Day was dead, missing or wounded. There were 6,000 American casualties (of whom 700 were airborne troops), which constituted more than half the total Allied casualties on D-Day. By the end of July the Americans were the majority Allied force in France with 980,000 troops, compared with 660,000 British. By Victory in Europe (VE) Day, 3 million US troops were fighting on the Continent.

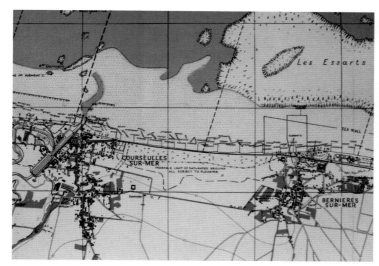

◀ Insignia of the 50th Northumbrian Division which went ashore on Gold Beach. (Author)

◀ Wartime map of Juno Beach showing beach obstacles. The Canadian 3rd Division landed here, including the Royal Winnipeg Rifles and Regina Rifles at Courseulles-sur-Mer (left) and the Queen's Own Rifles of Canada at Bernières-sur-Mer (right).

H-Hour at Sword Beach was designated as 0530hrs. The shore bombardment was delivered by two battleships, HMS *Warspite* and *Ramilles*, the monitor HMS *Roberts*, cruisers HMS *Mauritius*, *Arethusa*, *Frobisher* and *Danae*, and the Polish ORP *Dragon*, and thirteen destroyers including two from the Polish Navy (plus two more as part of the covering force) and the Norwegian HMNS *Svenner*. The increased naval support on Sword was due to the larger number of German batteries in the sector. At 0537hrs, while the smaller vessels headed towards their bombarding stations, the *Svenner* was hit amidships by German torpedo boats on patrol from Le Havre with the loss of one officer and thirty-three crew. At 0650hrs the self-propelled guns of the 3rd Infantry Division opened fire from their landing craft at a range of 10,000yd (9.1km). At 0725hrs the British 3rd Infantry Division and 27th Armoured Brigade, eighteen minutes later than scheduled, went ashore with forty DD tanks (six, including two which were rammed by out-of-control landing craft, were lost) and flame-throwers, and came under mortar fire. The first wave of infantry, the 8th Infantry Brigade Group, the 1st Battalion of the South Lancashire Regiment and the 2nd East Yorkshires, arrived to find that the first of the 13th/18th Royal Hussars' DD tanks were already ashore and firing at German strongpoints. At 0750hrs Nos 4 and 10 (Free French) Commando landed and there was heavy fighting on the beach.

At 0821hrs flail tanks from the 22nd Dragoons and the Westminster Dragoons

◄ German fighter ace *Oberstleutnant* Josef 'Pips' Priller. Priller claimed his 97th and 98th victories, a P-47 and a P-51, on 7 June, and his 100th victory came on 15 June when he shot down a B-24 Liberator of the 492nd Bomb Group. His wingman, Heinz Wodarczyk, was killed on 1 January 1945. Priller survived the war with a total of 101 victories. (Bundesarchiv)

Did You Know?

By D+50 631,000 personnel, 153,000 vehicles and 689,000 tons of stores, plus 68,000 tons of fuel and oil, were delivered to the bridgehead.

cleared paths through minefields, and exits from the beach were opened more quickly than on any other beach. By 0835hrs three beach exits had been cleared of the enemy. At 0930hrs Hermanville was taken, the Riva Bella casino strongpoint was captured by the Free French but heavy German opposition halted the advance. With a fast incoming tide the beach became congested and the reserve brigades were held up, but during 1000–1200hrs the German strongpoints inland were gradually overcome. At 1100hrs the British 185th Brigade, whose mission was to capture Caen, was ashore and formed up, but traffic jams kept them from advancing until 1230hrs. German Panzers were reported north of Caen at 1215hrs: the 21st Panzer Group of 20,000 men, commanded by Major General Edgar Feuchtinger, had disobeyed orders and attacked between Caen and Bayeux.

Further landings were made at 1200hrs on Juno Beach, and at 1300hrs on Gold Beach all of the 50th (Northumbrian) Division were ashore. The British 185th Brigade moved inland from Sword at 1230hrs and, an hour later, Brigadier Lord Lovat's 1st Special Service Brigade reached Pegasus Bridge en route to help other units of the Airborne Division. At 1400hrs there was fighting on Périers Ridge overlooking Sword, which was cleared by the 2nd King's Shropshire Light Infantry, even though their tank support failed to turn up. From 1400hrs onwards the whole of Canadian 3rd Division was ashore on Juno Beach and rapid advances were made inland. The troops joined with Gold Beach to the west, and a reserve brigade with four regiments of artillery and a third armoured regiment were able to expand the bridgehead. Forces from Gold Beach finally captured Le Hamel at 1600hrs and 231st Brigade moved on to Arromanches. At about that time 69th Brigade made contact with a battalion of the German 915th Regiment and the 352nd Fusilier Battalion as well as two anti-tank batteries in the area between Villiers-le-Sec and Bazenville. After a stiff fight the Germans were driven across the River Seulles. Meanwhile, 9th Brigade moved inland from Sword Beach and 185th Brigade repulsed an attack by the 21st Panzer Division at Périers Ridge, destroying sixteen tanks in the process. At 1800hrs the Canadian 9th Brigade reached Bény, but the British advance by the 185th Brigade on Caen was halted at Biéville, 3 miles (5km) short of the city. At 1900hrs, with a battle group of tanks and a battalion of infantry, 21st Panzer Division mounted a massive counter-attack, but the drive failed just short of the cliffs at Luc-sur-Mer with the loss of thirteen tanks. At 2000hrs the Allies captured Bénouville and a counter-attack was made towards the sea between Sword and Juno beaches. The 'Hillman' strongpoint was finally secured after a long battle and, by 2030hrs, the 56th and 151st Brigades from Gold

Did You Know?
On 17 July Rommel was badly wounded when two RAF Typhoons attacked a convoy of German staff cars during the retreat from Caen. Though not a conspirator in the July Plot against Hitler, the plotters had considered him as a potential Chief of State. The Fuhrer offered him a choice of suicide or a public trial which would involve his wife and son. He chose suicide and died on 14 October and was buried with full military honours at the age of 53.

had reached the outskirts of Bayeux and the Caen–Bayeux road. By 2100hrs, the Hampshires had cleared the radar station at Ste-Côme-de-Fresné and had taken Arromanches. At the same time a group of more than 250 Allied gliders flew in and deterred the German attack.

By nightfall British forces on Sword had linked up with Canadians at Juno Beach. All told, 29,000 had landed on Sword with fewer than 1,000 casualties and 47 Royal Marine Commando were ready to take Port-en-Bessin the following day. By midnight, 24,970 troops had been landed on Gold, for a loss of 413 killed, wounded or missing. Altogether, 21,400 men, 3,200 vehicles and 2,100 tons of stores were landed on Juno for the loss of 359 killed and 715 wounded. Twelve exit lanes were clear and Canadian follow-up units – the 7th Brigade on the right, the 9th on the left – were past the assault troops, as planned, and heading for Caen. 21,500 men of the 3rd Canadian Division and 2nd Armoured Brigade and British troops stormed 7 miles (11km) inland. The Canadians made the most progress of all the beaches and at nightfall were within sight of Caen, while two battalions were only 3 miles (5km) from its north-west outskirts. However, the original aim of capturing Carpiquet airfield was not achieved and no link-up had yet been made with Sword Beach to the east, where 6 square miles (18 square km) of beach was under British control. Two days later Omaha and Gold beachheads joined, and Utah made contact with Omaha on 10 June, after which General Montgomery established his HQ in Normandy. On 12 June Carentan was liberated, joining up Utah and Omaha landings and allowing all five beachheads to join up.

In the period 6 June to 31 August, 21st Army Group suffered 83,825 casualties.

From 7 June onwards 65,000 men and 19,000 vehicles left Weymouth and Portland to reinforce the initial landings. The first RAF base was established on French soil and British 7th Armoured attacked towards Villers-Bocage. By this time 330,000 men and 50,000 vehicles were ashore. As US VII Corps fought its way across the Cotentin Peninsula, the rest of US First Army thrust forward around St Lô. Further east the British and Canadian Corps of British Second Army battled their way around Caen against fierce German counter-attacks. By the end of June 875,000 men had landed in Normandy, sixteen divisions each for the American and British armies. Although the Allies were well established on the coast and possessed all the Cotentin Peninsular, the Americans had still not taken St Lô, nor had the British and Canadians captured the town of Caen, originally a target for D-Day.

German resistance, particularly around Caen, was ferocious, but more and more well-trained German troops were thrown into the battle, so that when the Allies did break out of Normandy the defenders lost heavily and lacked the men to stop the Allied forces from almost reaching the borders of Germany. The German Army should have taken the advice of Field Marshal Gerd von Rundstedt, Commander-in-Chief West, on 10 June when Field Marshal Wilhelm Keitel, head of Armed Forces High Command, ringing from Paris in panic, asked 'What shall we do?' and was told 'Make peace you fool'.

➤ A desolate French woman sits amongst the debris of her Normandy village home. Chief of the Imperial General Staff, General Sir Alan Brooke, noted that, 'The French population did not seem in any way pleased to see us arrive as a victorious army to liberate France. They had been quite content as they were and we were bringing war and desolation to their country.' (IWM)

◄ Arlette Gondrée, owner and proprietor of the Café Gondrée, who was 3 years old when Pegasus Bridge was taken, and a British war veteran being interviewed by an Australian TV crew in 2004. Arlette, sister Georgette and their parents Georges and Thérèse hid in the cellar of their home on the night of 5 June 1944. The dining room was used as an operating theatre. (Author)

▲ View of Arromanches reflected in a carousel on the shore. (Author)

◀◀ A joyful French woman in Gisors welcomes Allied troops. (IWM)

◀ Sherman Grizzly tank T146929 AKILLA at the Land Warfare Museum, IWM Duxford. (Author)

◄ HMS *Belfast*, which is permanently moored on the Thames near London's Tower Bridge. (Author)

▲ Lest We Forget. Memorial behind a draw on Utah Beach on the D421. (Author)

◀ 1st Lieutenant Lester Weiss' gravestone at Ste-Laurent-sur-Mer Cemetery. Weiss, who was from Yonkers, New York, was the navigator on B-24 Liberator *Mean Widdle Kid* in the 487th Bomb Group at Lavenham and was one of seven men killed on 11 May 1944 when the bomber was shot down at Orgeres. (Author)

▲ In memoria.
(Author)

▲ Map on the clifftop overlooking
Arromanches. (Author)

 Memorial stained-glass window with badges of the Allied nations in Portsmouth Cathedral. (Author)

 Memorial stained-glass window to Admiral Sir Bertram Ramsay, the Allied Naval Commander, in Portsmouth Cathedral. (Author)

In the Second World War, General Montgomery used a Fordson 'map caravan', built by the British Trailer Company, Manchester, and delivered to St Paul's School on 17 April 1944. He also used two Italian caravans captured from Maresciallo Giovanni Messe, commander of the First Italian Army in Tunisia and the vehicle liberated near Benghazi from Generale di Corpo d'Armata Annibale Bergonzoli, commander of XXIII Corps during the North Africa campaign. Montgomery always kept a portrait of Rommel in his caravan (left) and here in his bedroom caravan is a photograph of Field Marshal Walther Model, who opposed his forces during Market Garden and the abortive attempt to capture Arnhem Bridge in September 1944. 'Monty' was allowed to keep the vehicles during his lifetime and they were stored in a barn at his home at Isington Mill in Hampshire until four months after his death in March 1976. Today, all three caravans are on display at the Land Warfare Museum, IWM Duxford. (Author)

➤ Monty's bedroom caravan was remounted on a Mack chassis (pictured) following its capture in Tunisia in May 1943 and the office caravan was remounted on a Leyland chassis after capture at Beda Fomm, Libya, in February 1941. (Author)

➤➤ Normandy memorial window in Portsmouth Cathedral. (Author)

➤➤➤ The panel at the foot of the Normandy memorial window. (Author)

▲ The Allied war cemetery at Ste-Laurent-sur-Mer, which contains 9,286 burials, 307 of whom are unknown, who were killed during and after the Omaha landings. (Author)

▲ The Overlord Embroidery at the D-Day Museum at Southsea, near Portsmouth, which tells the story of D-Day in thirty-four panels. (Author)

➤ General Theodore Roosevelt Jr, the 4th Division's assistant commander, died of a heart attack on 12 July 1944, the day he was due to take command of his own division. Awarded the Medal of Honor, he lies buried at Ste-Laurent-sur-Mer, beside the grave of his reinterred brother, Quentin, killed in 1918. Medal of Honor recipients' headstones are lettered in gold. Thirty other pairs of brothers lie side by side, as do a father and son. (Author)

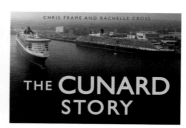